Flickering
Philippians

Noel and Denise Enete

WAVE
Study
Bible

Published by WAVE Study Bible, Inc., *wavestudybible.com*
Available from Amazon, *amazon.com*
Edition 1.0.0

ISBN 978-0-9791595-6-5

Printed and bound in the United States of America

Table of Contents

"If you know
God, you start
discerning what
His values are."

The Authors

Preface

These *Flicker Study Guides* have been carefully ordered so the first few study guides contain passages that are the simplest to *Flicker* and contain the most important spiritual truth. As you progress through the *Guides* the passages get more challenging and fill out your grasp of the full counsel of God.

These first passages are all narratives (i.e. stories) which lend themselves best to the open ended creative *Flicker* steps. Also, these first few *Flicker Study Guides* give you the best chance to watch Jesus, who is God, in action. As you watch and learn what He does and responds to, you have the best chance to get to know what God is like and trust Him as a real friend.

This *Flicker Study Guide* shifts from passages that are narratives to passages that are logical in nature. When *Flickering* logical literature you often encounter a verse that is already in the form of a principle—e.g. in the form of a *Lesson*. For example, *"Rejoice in the Lord always" (Philippians 4:4a)*. This is a *Lesson* already, so you repeat the verse in your list of *Lessons*. Then as you keep looking at the verse, you keep looking for what is unusual and write what you continue to learn. For example, you can also learn that "God doesn't want us to always focus on the problem" and "Rejoicing is not an isolated event. God sees it as an attitude that goes with you throughout the day."

The content in *Philippians* is wonderful *Foundational* truth to begin your individual Bible studying journey with. Since it is written to believers who are in the church age, its application to our lives is straight forward and it deals with foundational Christian attitudes like humility, pure thought life, and unselfishness. It even has one of the great Bible prayers in *Philippians 1:9-11* that you can any time pray for yourself directly back to God.

Enjoy this guide as it helps you *Flicker* the entire book of *Philippians*.

Organization of the Book

This book takes you through several passages that are fundamental to faith in Christ and helps you decide how your values may differ from His.

The format of this book encourages you to write out what you notice in the passages and respond to God accordingly. Then as you explore these passages, also be alert to notice what you can learn about what God is like.

If you are not familiar with *Flicker Bible Study,* an explanation of the steps and an example of a *Flickered* passage follows.

How To Flicker the Bible

Facts

In the *Facts* panel, make a list of the *Facts* you see in the passage. You don't have to list all the details. Just try and find the main points. You can use the same words as are in the passage. You will usually get somewhere around four to six *Facts*.

Lessons

In the *Lessons* panel, look over the list of facts and see what you can learn from the passage.

- Is there an example to follow?
- Is there a behavior to stop or start?
- Is there a comfort to accept?

Also, consider what you can learn about God from this passage? What does He value? What does He respond to? What pleases Him? You don't have to find a *Lesson* from every verse. Usually you will get one or two *Lessons* from a passage.

Challenges

In the *Challenges* panel, turn each *Lesson* you surfaced into a question that *Challenges* you. Listen for God to speak to you. He may not speak to you through every verse, but He will speak to you. You will normally get the same number of *Challenges* as *Lessons*.

Response

In the *Response* panel, consider what God is saying to you through this passage and decide how you will respond. Write out your *Response* as a two or three sentence prayer.

Be heartfelt and honest with God. If needed, put "training wheels" on your *Response*: "Lord help me to want this." Better to be honest and ask for help, than promise behavior you are not ready to keep.

Example: Psalm 121

To get an idea how to fill in the panels, the following pages present *Psalm 121 Flickered*. This is a guide to help you understand what kind of item goes in each panel.

More items are included in each panel than you would normally write out in the study of a passage. More are included to give you a better idea what goes in each panel.

For more explanation of *Flicker Bible Study* see our book, *Flickering the Bible: Desire-powered Inductive Bible Study*.

Example Passage

Psalms 121:1 I lift up my eyes to the mountains; From where shall my help come?

Psalms 121:2 My help [comes] from the LORD, Who made heaven and earth.

Psalms 121:3 He will not allow your foot to slip; He who keeps you will not slumber.

Psalms 121:4 Behold, He Who keeps Israel Will neither slumber nor sleep.

Psalms 121:5 The LORD is your keeper; the LORD is your shade on your right hand;

Psalms 121:6 The sun will not smite you by day, Nor the moon by night.

Psalms 121:7 The LORD will protect you from all evil; He will keep your soul.

Psalms 121:8 The Lord will guard your going out and your coming in From this time forth and forever. (NASB)

F LCR FACTS

I look up and wonder where my help will come from.

My help comes from God who made heaven and earth

God won't let me fall because He is always watching, He doesn't sleep

He keeps Israel and doesn't sleep or even slumber

The Lord keeps me and shades me at my right hand

The Lord protects me from evil He is keeping my soul safe

FL**CR** LESSONS

There are times we know we need help beyond ourselves

Help comes from God Who created heaven and earth and is alert and ready to help

God is constantly watching, ready to catch me before I fall

He can be so attentive because He never sleep or slumbers

God "keeps" Israel; God "keeps" me. Keeping me means He observes me, guards me, takes care of me, maintains me, retains me in His possession.

FL**C**R CHALLENGES

Am I humble enough to seek help when I need it?

Do I go to God for help, or something else?

Do I trust God to "keep" me?

Am I willing to learn what God considers "falling" instead of assuming falling means failure.

FL**C**R RESPONSES

Lord, help me to be more aware of Your help and presence.

Help me see my relationship with You from Your perspective.

Passage 1—**Philippians 1:1-6**

Philippians 1:1 Paul and Timothy, bond-servants of Christ Jesus, To all the saints in Christ Jesus who are in Philippi, including the overseers and deacons:

Philippians 1:2 Grace to you and peace from God our Father and the Lord Jesus Christ.

Philippians 1:3 I thank my God in all my remembrance of you,

Philippians 1:4 always offering prayer with joy in my every prayer for you all,

Philippians 1:5 in view of your participation in the gospel from the first day until now.

Philippians 1:6 [For I am] confident of this very thing, that He who began a good work in you will perfect it until the day of Christ Jesus. (NASB1995)

Paul thanks God when he remembers the Philippians.

God begins a good work in us when we accept
Christ.

Am I focused on the good work God is
accomplishing in me since I accepted Christ?

Commentary

Do you realize that God has started a good work in you? Did you also realize that He is going to perfect it when Christ comes back? Wow! Think about that. Presently, we struggle in our faith to stay focused. But, God will bring it all together when Christ comes back. Until then, what we do ends up working for or against this good work. The day of Christ Jesus will be a joyous day. But on that day will God find us focused on Him, and His will, or distracted and working in the wrong direction?

This passage tells us that Paul became joyful when he thought about the Philippian believers. Can you think of any servants of God who become joyful thinking about you? Can you think of any pastors who thank God for you because of your participation in the gospel?

Participating in the gospel, whether it be manual labor behind the scenes, or speaking up front, is possible for almost everyone. If you are housebound, participation might be keeping up on the needs of the ministry and praying. There is almost no better gift than having someone devoted to praying for you daily.

Make it your goal to participate in the gospel which will accomplish several things. First, it will help you stay focused on God's purpose for you on earth. You will be cooperating with Him as He perfects the good work He started in you. Secondly, it will strengthen your relationships with other servants of Christ. You will have the chance to bring joy to someone else, which will bring joy to you. And thirdly, you will have even more joy at the day of Christ Jesus because you will be found working and focused on Him.

What God is Like

- *1. God is patient.* He begins a good work but doesn't have to see the finished product until Christ comes.

- *2. God is a team player.* He allows us to participate in the gospel.

- *3. God does things well.* He will perfect the good work He started.

Philippians 1:7 For it is only right for me to feel this way about you all, because I have you in my heart, since both in my imprisonment and in the defense and confirmation of the gospel, you all are partakers of grace with me.

Philippians 1:8 For God is my witness, how I long for you all with the affection of Christ Jesus.

Philippians 1:9 And this I pray, that your love may abound still more and more in real knowledge and all discernment,

Philippians 1:10 so that you may approve the things that are excellent, in order to be sincere and blameless until the day of Christ;

Philippians 1:11 having been filled with the fruit of righteousness which [comes] through Jesus Christ, to the glory and praise of God. (NASB1995)

Paul has the Philippians in his heart.

God is watching us (like a loving Parent) because He cares.

Do I live like God is watching me or do I put Him out of my mind?

Commentary

"…God is our witness…." (Philippians 1:8)

If your first impression is negative when you hear that God is watching you, be careful. Your view of authority might be negative and might be spilling over onto God who is the One who cares about you. God is watching us like a loving Parent because He cares. He can beam with pride, thinking, "Well done My child," or watch in dismay as we forsake Him and His instructions. He places a great value on love and has demonstrated it as He sacrificed His only Son for us. Now He wants us to follow His lead about how to love.

So why is it important for us to love with real knowledge and discernment? Maybe because we tend to confuse love with fantasy at times. I'm sure I could find some women who think they "love" Brad Pitt, and some men who think they "love" Jennifer Aniston, even though they have never met them. Granted they may have followed their career, read all about them, and are sure they "know" them. But if they finally met them and told them they loved them, Brad and Jennifer would probably think their sentiment was shallow and untested. They love Brad and Jennifer's image, they don't really know *them*.

We can be that way with God. We might think we love God, even if we don't really know Him. We make up our version of who we think He is—two parts Santa Claus and one part Terminator. But, our love of Him will get tested. If we don't love Him with a real knowledge of Him, we can easily misunderstand His actions because He is not being consistent with our fantasy version of Him.

Once we start loving God according to real knowledge of Him, discernment (the application of knowledge) follows. If you know God, you start discerning what His values are. You start to see things from His perspective. Things start to make sense. You start to value what He values. You approve of excellent things like He does.

If you go through your life wanting excellent things you become sincere and blameless since you recognize what is excellent. This puts you on the path to righteousness which brings glory to God. All of this begins by getting to know God and loving Him for Who He really is.

What God is Like

- *1. God is an involved Parent.* He watches us and gives instructions, protection and love to help us.

- *2. God wants us to know Who He really is.* He wants a real relationship with us.

- *3. God wants the best for us.* He wants us to go for excellent things and be blameless.

- *4. God is pleased with us, even in our fallen, forgiven state.*

Philippians 1:12   Now I want you to know, brethren, that my circumstances have turned out for the greater progress of the gospel,

Philippians 1:13   so that my imprisonment in [the cause of] Christ has become well known throughout the whole praetorian guard and to everyone else,

Philippians 1:14   and that most of the brethren, trusting in the Lord because of my imprisonment, have far more courage to speak the word of God without fear.

Philippians 1:15   Some, to be sure, are preaching Christ even from envy and strife, but some also from good will;

Philippians 1:16   the latter [do it] out of love, knowing that I am appointed for the defense of the gospel;

Philippians 1:17   the former proclaim Christ out of selfish ambition rather than from pure motives, thinking to cause me distress in my imprisonment.

Philippians 1:18   What then? Only that in every way, whether in pretense or in truth, Christ is proclaimed; and in this I rejoice. Yes, and I will rejoice,

Philippians 1:19   for I know that this will turn out for my deliverance through your prayers and the provision of the Spirit of Jesus Christ,

Philippians 1:20   according to my earnest expectation and hope, that I will not be put to shame in anything, but [that] with all boldness, Christ will even now, as always, be exalted in my body, whether by life or by death.

Philippians 1:21   For to me, to live is Christ and to die is gain. (NASB1995)

His circumstances are helping the progress of the gospel.

Rejoicing in our circumstances is a concerted choice. Paul chooses to rejoice because he believes God can further the gospel message even if he is in prison or betrayed by others.

FLCR CHALLENGES

Am I choosing to believe and rejoice in my circumstances?

FLCR RESPONSES

Commentary

"I will not be put to shame in anything" (Philippians 1:19)

That is quite a statement. Paul was in prison. Most people feel ashamed when they end up in prison. On top of that, some of his "friends" were betraying him in his absence. They were preaching the gospel in order to get ahead of him. It would be easy to feel a little embarrassed and betrayed in all the chaos.

But what does Paul conclude? That God is able to advance the gospel even in betrayal and chaos. Paul seemed to know that he couldn't control other people's motives and behavior so he focused on what he could control, his own attitude and behavior. He chose to rejoice regardless of the other people's motives and behavior because God is bigger. He had confidence that God would deliver him just the way he expected to be delivered. His focus was on God's ability, so he could rejoice.

Paul was confident that Christ was the answer to his problems. He said, *"I know that this will turn out for my deliverance through your prayers and the help of the Spirit of Jesus Christ" (Philippians 1:19)* Do you have Paul's sense of confidence that your problems *will* be addressed by Christ? If you have that confidence, your life will help the progress of the gospel. Your attitude will naturally shine the spotlight on Christ, your hope. Like Paul, you will turn to Christ in prayer and expect His help as you do your part to address your problems. If you are confident that help will come from Christ, you will focus on Him.

But, what if you aren't so confident? What or whom do you turn to with your problems? Some turn to alcohol, or sleep, or TV, or food, or shopping, or sports, or pornography. Paul turned to Christ, but he didn't just passively wait. He put his effort into his attitude. He was determined to rejoice. He was determined to exalt Christ in his body. He was determined to be bold, despite his problems. He was so focused on Christ, it was irrelevant whether he lived or died. Talk about getting "above" your problems! He had the "big picture" so he could rejoice in what God was doing, despite his problems.

Do you think God will only use you if you are perfect? Paul was convinced that God would use selfish sinners for His work, as long as they were proclaiming the message of Christ. God is a patient, long suffering Father. If we speak the truth about His Son, He can use us, warts and all.

Paul knew to put his effort into his attitude and behavior. He rejoiced that God was advancing His gospel even in the chaos. It takes a lot of determination to keep our attitude in check. He did not try to control his imprisonment or the competing preachers. He trusted God to change his circumstances according to His will. He could rejoice because He believed God was in control and working His will even through his problems. We can waste a lot of energy trying to control our circumstances when we should be praying and trusting God for that. He wants us to control our attitude instead.

What God is Like

- *1. God is flexible.* He is willing to use sinners to spread the good news about the gospel.
- *2. God carries the heavy load.* He is in charge of the big picture, He wants us to be in charge of our attitude and behavior.
- *3. God is creative.* He can take our problems and use them to further the gospel if we trust Him.

Philippians 2:1 Therefore if there is any encouragement in Christ, if there is any consolation of love, if there is any fellowship of the Spirit, if any affection and compassion,

Philippians 2:2 make my joy complete by being of the same mind, maintaining the same love, united in spirit, intent on one purpose.

Philippians 2:3 Do nothing from selfishness or empty conceit, but with humility of mind regard one another as more important than yourselves;

Philippians 2:4 do not [merely] look out for your own personal interests, but also for the interests of others.

Philippians 2:5 Have this attitude in yourselves which was also in Christ Jesus,

Philippians 2:6 who, although He existed in the form of God, did not regard equality with God a thing to be grasped,

Philippians 2:7 but emptied Himself, taking the form of a bond-servant, [and] being made in the likeness of men.

Philippians 2:8 Being found in appearance as a man, He humbled Himself by becoming obedient to the point of death, even death on a cross.

Philippians 2:9 For this reason also, God highly exalted Him, and bestowed on Him the name which is above every name,

Philippians 2:10 so that at the name of Jesus EVERY KNEE WILL BOW, of those who are in heaven and on earth and under the earth,

Philippians 2:11 and that every tongue will confess that Jesus Christ is Lord, to the glory of God the Father. (NASB1995)

FLCR **FACTS**

If there is...

...any encouragement in Christ

...any consolation of love

...any fellowship of the Spirit

...any affection and compassion

We have the ability to be united with others in thought, love and purpose because we have access to Christ's love, encouragement, fellowship and compassion.

Am I of the same mind, spirit, love and purpose with other brothers and sisters in Christ?

FLCR RESPONSES

Commentary

Did you know the Bible says that everyone can become great? It says that the road to greatness is through servanthood, and everyone can be a servant.

If you want to become great, God says to put your effort into serving the needs of others as Christ modeled for us. It takes humility, faith and obedience to take this route. It is not intuitive. Our culture says if you want to be great go to an Ivy League school and become rich in your selfish ambition. Who is right? Well, if you want to be "great" in this TEMPORARY culture, be rich. But, if you want to be great in God's ETERNAL culture, find it in servanthood.

For those who choose selfish ambition there is a heavy price tag. They will find that they are focused on themselves. They will never feel free the way they are hoping for, and none of their work transfers into eternity. Those who choose servanthood will find the freedom that comes with trusting God for their security and the satisfaction of focusing on, and helping, others. There is freedom and joy in obedience. God rewards those who don't selfishly step on others trying to find security and greatness. Christ is our example. He did not grasp at greatness and the security of being equal with God, but obeyed God the Father by becoming a bond-servant to Him.

By the way, being a bond-servant is different than being a doormat. It takes strength to serve. You can't give out of your poverty. A servant needs to take care of their basic needs like diet, exercise and sleep in order to have the most to give. Those who don't take care of themselves burn out and wonder why they feel like a doormat. Those who are co-dependently giving, need to control the outcome and are too focused on manipulating others to get the outcome they want. A bond-servant is focused on God, willing to obey Him, yet responsible for taking care of their own basic needs so God can use them the most. Instead of a co-dependent need to twist another's life, a bond-servant allows God to guide them. God can bring unity of purpose when we trust Him.

Unity is a fun experience for those who choose to be of the same mind, love, Spirit and purpose. We find Christ's affection, compassion, encouragement, love, and fellowship as we study His Word. What a pay off! But, having God's Word without reading it is like having a check for $10 million dollars but never cashing it. In God's economy, servanthood leads to greatness.

What God is Like

- *1. God is fair.* Greatness comes through servanthood so all can achieve it.

- *2. God provides* the encouragement, love, affection, fellowship, and compassion we need as we spend time with Him in His Word.

- *3. God allows us to choose.* He does not over-control us. He is not co-dependent, needing us to respond a certain way so He can feel OK.

- *4. God works with us,* guiding us through the consequences of our choices.

- *5. God loves unity and fellowship.*

- *6. God loves to encourage through Christ's example.*

- *7. God is affectionate.*

- *8. God is compassionate.*

Philippians 3:3 for we are the [true] circumcision, who worship in the Spirit of God and glory in Christ Jesus and put no confidence in the flesh,

Philippians 3:4 although I myself might have confidence even in the flesh. If anyone else has a mind to put confidence in the flesh, I far more:

Philippians 3:5 circumcised the eighth day, of the nation of Israel, of the tribe of Benjamin, a Hebrew of Hebrews; as to the Law, a Pharisee;

Philippians 3:6 as to zeal, a persecutor of the church; as to the righteousness which is in the Law, found blameless.

Philippians 3:7 But whatever things were gain to me, those things I have counted as loss for the sake of Christ.

Philippians 3:8 More than that, I count all things to be loss in view of the surpassing value of knowing Christ Jesus my Lord, for whom I have suffered the loss of all things, and count them but rubbish so that I may gain Christ,

Philippians 3:9 and may be found in Him, not having a righteousness of my own derived from [the] Law, but that which is through faith in Christ, the righteousness which [comes] from God on the basis of faith, (NASB1995)

The Jews are the true circumcision.

You don't need to have your own righteousness to gain Christ as your Lord.

Is my confidence in my ability to be a righteous rule keeper, or in Christ's work?

Commentary

When it came to prestige and credentials Paul had arrived. He was theoretically the perfect Jew. He was from the tribe of Benjamin (Benjamin and Joseph were Jacob's favorite sons), he was born into a pure Hebrew family, and had reached the summit of religious education by becoming a Pharisee. But, now he was calling all of his religious triumphs worthless, in comparison to gaining Christ Jesus as his Lord. Instead of excelling in religion, he wanted to excel in relationship with Christ.

How about you? Do you think you need to "bring something to the table" so Christ will value a relationship with you? We need to get our eyes off ourselves and onto Christ, like Paul did. It is a wake up call. God doesn't want us to work our way to heaven, but He does want a relationship with us which shifts our focus off ourselves and onto a transformative relationship with Christ.

Our sense of what makes us righteous changes. Instead of trying to make ourselves righteous by keeping all the rules, we realize that Christ *is* righteous and we become righteous by identifying with Him. It is a very different focus. Instead of obeying to *earn* something (which causes either pride or fear), we obey out of love and respect for Christ as our righteousness. When we fall short, we accept His forgiveness—it is all about relationship.

Do you think your best assets make you valuable to God, or is it your faith in Christ's assets that God values?

What God is Like

- *1. God loves us.* We don't have to earn His love. By faith we accept it.

- *2. God wants a relationship with us.* He wants us to accept His love and not try to earn it.

- *3. God likes good behavior.* He will make us righteous through our faith in His efforts.

Philippians 3:17 Brethren, join in following my example, and observe those who walk according to the pattern you have in us.

Philippians 3:18 For many walk, of whom I often told you, and now tell you even weeping, [that they are] enemies of the cross of Christ,

Philippians 3:19 whose end is destruction, whose god is [their] appetite, and [whose] glory is in their shame, who set their minds on earthly things.

Philippians 3:20 For our citizenship is in heaven, from which also we eagerly wait for a Savior, the Lord Jesus Christ;

Philippians 3:21 who will transform the body of our humble state into conformity with the body of His glory, by the exertion of the power that He has even to subject all things to Himself. (NASB1995)

Paul wants his brethren to...

...follow his example.

You don't need to have your own righteousness to gain Christ as your Lord.

Is my confidence in my ability to be a righteous rule keeper, or in Christ's work?

Commentary

Whose example are you following? Paul instructs us to follow his example and warns us not to follow those who walk as enemies of the cross of Christ. Wait, what? Christ has enemies?

He sure does. So, how do we recognize these enemies? Well, we can distinguish them by the way they think and the way they behave. They want to be boss. They think their desires and choices are more important than God's desires and choices for them.

Their behavior is also a *tell*. Instead of being ashamed of their sin, they revel in it. They glory in their shame. They have the right to choose and they glory in that power. They may talk like they are Christians, but they don't follow Christ. They follow their own appetite and it will lead them to destruction.

Following Christ, on the other hand, leads us to focus on heaven where we are citizens. We are not citizens of the world. We eagerly wait for our Savior, the Lord Jesus Christ to take us there. We are trusting Him to make that happen. He promises to transform our humble bodies to be like His glorious body. We won't always be flawed.

Our job is to follow God's example, know our citizenship is not really here, and eagerly wait for Him. We have a lot to look forward to!

What God is Like

- *1. God is long suffering.* Have you ever been accused of evil when you were doing an act of kindness? It causes suffering, right? God's enemies accuse Him of evil day in and day out and yet He is long suffering. He is willing to have enemies without immediately destroying them. God is willing to suffer and be patient while He works His plan for us, and His enemies, if they are willing to accept it.

- *2. God is a teacher at heart.* He gives us written instructions and examples to follow and a Holy Spirit to guide us.

- *3. God is clear.* He warns. He does not want any to be destroyed so He provided clear instructions.

Philippians 4:4 Rejoice in the Lord always; again I will say, rejoice!

Philippians 4:5 Let your gentle [spirit] be known to all men. The Lord is near.

Philippians 4:6 Be anxious for nothing, but in everything by prayer and supplication with thanksgiving let your requests be made known to God.

Philippians 4:7   And the peace of God, which surpasses all comprehension, will guard your hearts and your minds in Christ Jesus. (NASB1995)

We should always rejoice in the Lord

There is never a time where rejoicing IN THE LORD is inappropriate.

Am I willing to rejoice in the Lord, no matter how bad things are going, because I believe He is good and able?

Commentary

"Rejoice in the Lord always; again I will say, rejoice." *(Philippians 4:4)* So much good can come from turning your thinking from the problems to being thankful for God's guidance. Once you start seeing His loving hand in situations you don't understand He can guide you.

However, this verse can also be applied in a harmful way.

I [D] once heard of a Christian family who had a child commit suicide. In the face of this trauma they didn't ask God to help them understand why their child felt hopeless. They didn't look for how to improve the factors that led to this catastrophe. Rather, they just went passive and used this verse to avoid any responsibility on their part. After all they were obeying God and rejoicing always. They did not pray for wisdom, or look for anything that might need to get addressed in the family. They just avoided their problems and rejoiced.

This caused another one of their children to despair. Who could live *this kind of* Christian life that avoids problems? So they also committed suicide. This got the parent's attention and they finally started looking to God and asking what was not working in their family. What they did wrong was to use this verse to avoid their problems.

If they had rejoiced because the God of the universe loved them and would do the right thing for their deceased child and would thankfully give them the wisdom they needed to change what needed to change, they could have found some of God's peace and that would have made more sense to their second child.

We are partners with God. Whenever we lay all the responsibility for our life on God, (I'll just rejoice and not change anything) or all the responsibility on ourselves (God won't help me, it's all up to me) we will be vulnerable for mood instability.

It is always appropriate to rejoice because He is sovereign, and just, and His love never fails. He is in control even when things seem to be going wrong. But rejoicing does not take the place of being responsible for what is going wrong in our life. We rejoice in God's control, but we pray for wisdom to discern our part in every situation. We are thankful that God will lead us as we consult Him in prayer.

This brings us peace. We are not alone in our problems. If we rejoice in the Lord, instead of our circumstances, we will not have unstable moods that go up and down. Our focus is on the Lord, not our circumstances. God is not asking us to rejoice in bad circumstances, He wants us to rejoice that He can see us through *even this*.

The trick is to *know God*. We know our problems and worries very well. If we don't really know God we won't be able to focus on Him in order to rejoice. We have to believe that He is good, and stronger, than our problems. That He will see us through. That His love never fails because He is good, not because we are good. That He has our back. This kind of *knowing God* guards our hearts and minds because we have ammunition for how to think about our situation. We know and believe Him when He says He will take care of us. That is why we rejoice. Then we address our problems with His guidance. There is no need for anxiety. He will see us through. Fretting stems from wanting our own way. Calmness comes when we know God enough to trust His way.

What God is Like

- *1. God cares how we feel.* He does not want us to suffer from anxiety. He wants us to feel good. Calm and peaceful.
- *2. God appreciates an attitude of thankfulness.* He wants us to thankfully pray to Him about what we want.
- *3. God wants us to realize He is a continual positive in our life no matter how things are going.*

Philippians 4:8   Finally, brethren, whatever is true, whatever is honorable, whatever is right, whatever is pure, whatever is lovely, whatever is of good repute, if there is any excellence and if anything worthy of praise, dwell on these things. (NASB1995)

Think on these things:

God cares about our thought life.

FLCR CHALLENGES

Am I working on what I think about?

FLCR RESPONSES

Commentary

God is asking us to think about lovely things in this verse. Does He just want us to blow sunshine around, not really in reality? No, notice that He says to think of lovely TRUE things *(whatever is true)*. He wants us in reality.

So where do we find material that is *true, honorable, right, pure, lovely, excellent, of good reputation and worthy of praise* to think about? First, we find it in God's Word. Then we find it when we look at life from God's perspective. He wants to transform us by changing how we think.

You might be tempted to think that transformation comes by changing how you behave—you just try harder and start behaving better. Well, good luck with that. The Bible says to *"be transformed by the renewing of your mind"* (Romans 12:2). Transformation happens when we change how we think about God, the world, the people around us, and ourselves. God wants us to think about all of these from His perspective. When we view life from His perspective we become less anxious. Our feelings and behavior follow our thinking.

God knows that how we think effects how we feel. He wants us to feel good, so He is prescribing what will help us feel better—a steady flow of good, true, thoughts. We won't find a steady flow of good thoughts in the newspaper or the evening news. But, you can find it in God's Word when He says *He is love* and *His love never fails,* or when He says *He is all powerful* and *can accomplish what concerns you today.* There is a reason He tells us to think about good, true things. That kind of thinking will transform us.

What God is Like

- *1. God is intimately involved in our life.* He cares what we think about. He wants us to feel good. He does not want us dwelling on scary and depressing things.

- *2. God is true, honorable, right, pure, lovely, of good reputation, excellent and worthy of praise.* We are helped by getting to know Him. He gives us food for thought.

Philippians 4:10 But I rejoiced in the Lord greatly, that now at last you have revived your concern for me; indeed, you were concerned [before,] but you lacked opportunity.

Philippians 4:11 Not that I speak from want, for I have learned to be content in whatever circumstances I am.

Philippians 4:12 I know how to get along with humble means, and I also know how to live in prosperity; in any and every circumstance I have learned the secret of being filled and going hungry, both of having abundance and suffering need.

Philippians 4:13 I can do all things through Him who strengthens me.

Philippians 4:18 But I have received everything in full and have an abundance; I am amply supplied, having received from Epaphroditus what you have sent, a fragrant aroma, an acceptable sacrifice, well-pleasing to God.

Philippians 4:19 And my God will supply all your needs according to His riches in glory in Christ Jesus. (NASB1995)

Paul rejoiced greatly in the Lord

Helping to meet a person's need, helps them rejoice and thank the Lord.

Do I realize it will most likely strengthen a person's relationship with God if I help them?

Commentary

Do you realize that God has started a good work in you? Did you also realize that He is going to perfect it when Christ comes back? Wow! Think about that. Presently, we struggle in our faith to stay focused. But, God will bring it all together when Christ comes back. Until then, what we do ends up working for or against this good work. The day of Christ Jesus will be a joyous day. But on that day will God find us focused on Him, and His will, or distracted and working in the wrong direction?

This passage tells us that Paul became joyful when he thought about the Philippian believers. Can you think of any servants of God who become joyful thinking about you? Can you think of any pastors who thank God for you because of your participation in the gospel?

Participating in the gospel, whether it be manual labor behind the scenes, or speaking up front, is possible for almost everyone. If you are housebound, participation might be keeping up on the needs of the ministry and praying. There is almost no better gift than having someone devoted to praying for you daily.

Make it your goal to participate in the gospel which will accomplish several things. First, it will help you stay focused on God's purpose for you on earth. You will be cooperating with Him as He perfects the good work He started in you. Secondly, it will strengthen your relationships with other servants of Christ. You will have the chance to bring joy to someone else, which will bring joy to you. And thirdly, you will have even more joy at the day of Christ Jesus because you will be found working and focused on Him.

What God is Like

- *1. God is patient.* He begins a good work but doesn't have to see the finished product until Christ comes.

- *2. God is a team player.* He allows us to participate in the gospel.

- *3. God does things well.* He will perfect the good work He started.

"Am I wise
in my own
eyes?"

the Authors

Appendix A
Answers

More answers are given below than you are expected to find when you study the passages. Most people find four to six *Facts*, one or two *Lessons*, one or two *Challenges*, and one *Response* when they study a passage. Extra answers are given here to help you better recognize *Facts, Lessons, Challenges*, and *Responses*.

Passage 1—Philippians 1:1-6

Facts

- Paul thanks God when he remembers the Philippians.
- Paul's prayers for them are always joyful.
- His prayers are joyful because of their participation in the gospel from the first day until now.
- He is confident about these things...
- ...that He Who began a good work in them,
- ...will perfect it,
- ...until the day of Christ Jesus.

Lessons

- God begins a good work in us when we accept Christ.
- God will perfect the good work in us over time. It will become perfect at the day of Christ Jesus.

Challenges

- Am I focused on the good work God is accomplishing in me since I accepted Christ?
- Am I cooperating with, or resisting, this good work that God is accomplishing in me?
- Do I realize God will perfect this good work in me over time?
- Do I realize God's work in me will be perfect at the day of Christ Jesus?
- Do I live like the day of Christ Jesus is a reality that is coming?

Responses

- Lord, thank You for beginning a good work in me when I accepted Christ as my Savior.
- Please help me to be focused on this work and cooperate with the direction You want me to go.
- Please forgive me when I buck You or work against You.
- Thank You that You will accomplish this work at the day of Christ Jesus, but help me to be wise and not make my life hard because of foolish choices that take me in the wrong direction.

Passage 2—Philippians 1:7-11

Facts

- Paul is confident about the Philippians.
- They have shared God's grace through Paul's imprisonment and the defense of the gospel.
- God is Paul's witness.
- Paul longs for them with the affection of Christ.
- Paul prays that their love may abound more and more...
- ...in real knowledge,
- ...in all discernment.
- So that...
- ...they will approve of excellent things.
- Then they...
- ...will be sincere and blameless until the day of Christ
- The Philippians will be filled with the fruit of righteousness.
- This fruit comes through Jesus Christ.
- This brings glory and praise to God.

Lessons

- God is watching us (like a loving Parent) because He cares.
- When you walk with Christ, His affection for others is contagious. His love grows within you.
- God wants your love to be discerning. He wants your love to be based in truth, not fantasy.
- If you are discerning you will love excellent things.
- Loving excellent things will keep you blameless until the day of Christ and fill you with the fruit of righteousness.
- The fruit of righteousness comes through Jesus Christ and brings glory and praise to God.

Challenges

- Do I live like God is watching me or do I put Him out of my mind?
- Do I believe He is fondly watching me because He cares and loves me?
- Am I walking closely enough with Christ so that His love is growing in me?
- Am I using Christ's love to love others?
- Is my love discerning?
- Is my love based in truth, or fantasy?
- Do I love excellent things?
- Is my love for excellent things keeping me blameless until the day of Christ?
- Am I growing in the fruit of righteousness?
- Do I look to Christ to gain the fruit of righteousness?
- Do I want to bring glory and praise to God? Am I looking to Christ to achieve this?

Responses

- Father, thank You for keeping Your eye on me.
- Thank You for caring.
- Please forgive me when I don't live like I care about You and what You want for me.
- Please help me live for You and make You proud.

Passage 3—Philippians 1:12-21

Facts

- Paul wants the brethren to know several things.
- His circumstances are helping the progress of the gospel.
- All the prison guards know he is in prison for the cause of Christ.
- Most of the brethren are trusting the Lord because of Paul's imprisonment.
- They have more courage to speak the word of God without fear.
- Some are preaching Christ from envy and strife.
- Some are preaching from good will.
- The latter preach out of love.
- They know Paul is appointed to defend the gospel.
- The former preach out of selfish ambition.
- They don't have pure motives.
- They try to cause Paul distress in his imprisonment.
- What is one to conclude?
- Whether in bad or good, Christ is preached.
- In this he rejoices.
- And he will rejoice.
- He knows this will end up delivering him through their prayers and the help of the Spirit of Jesus Christ.
- It will happen according to his earnest expectation and hope that he will not be put to shame in anything.
- He has boldness that Christ will even now, as always, be exalted in his body.
- Whether by life or by death,
- To him to live is Christ,
- To die is gain.

Lessons

- Rejoicing in our circumstances is a concerted choice. Paul chooses to rejoice because he believes God can further the gospel message even if he is in prison or betrayed by others.
- Our circumstances, no matter if they are good or bad, can help the progress of the gospel if our attitude shines the spotlight on Christ, our hope.
- When we walk with God our thinking changes. Paul did not fret over those who preached the gospel with selfish motives. He knew God was bigger than our sin and could use the message of the gospel no matter how sinful we are.

69

- When we have faith in God's message and power we can rise above our suffering and rejoice in what He is doing, even if we aren't delivered yet.
- If we focus on God's gospel message it overtakes our life. We start to see our whole life revolving around Christ. Living is about Christ. Dying is about Christ.

Challenges

- Am I choosing to believe and rejoice in my circumstances?
- Is my attitude about my circumstances helping the progress of the gospel?
- Do I focus on God and His ability, or on my suffering?
- Is my thinking changing as I walk with God?
- Am I able to "get above" my circumstances and see things from God's point of view?
- Do I need to be delivered before I rejoice, or do I allow my faith in God's message to enable me to rejoice?
- Is my whole life revolving around Christ? Is living and dying about Christ?

Responses

- Father, thank You that You have a plan and You are more powerful than my circumstances.
- Thank You that You can further the gospel if I'm willing to trust and follow You even in difficult circumstances.
- Please give me wisdom to think like You and the strength to choose to rejoice.
- May Your will be done in my life.

Passage 4—Philippians 2:1-11

Facts

- If there is...
- ...any encouragement in Christ
- ...any consolation of love
- ...any fellowship of the Spirit
- ...any affection and compassion,
- Make my joy complete by...
- ...being of the same mind
- ...maintaining the same love
- ...united in spirit
- ...intent on one purpose.
- Do nothing from...
- ...selfish ambition
- ...empty conceit.
- With humility...
- ...regard one another as more important than yourselves
- ...do not just look out for your own personal interests
- ...look out for the interest of others.

- Have the same attitude as Jesus...
- ...although He existed in the form of God
- ...He did not regard equality with God a thing to be grasped.
- ...Instead He emptied Himself
- ...taking on the form of a bond-servant
- ...being made in the likeness of man
- ...He humbled Himself by becoming obedient to death on a cross.
- For this reason God highly exalted Him
- God bestowed on Him the name which is above every name
- God gave Him that name so that...
- ...every knee in heaven and earth and under the earth will bow at the name of Jesus
- ...every tongue will confess that Jesus Christ is Lord.
- This brings glory to God the Father.

Lessons

- We have the ability to be united with others in thought, love and purpose because we have access to Christ's love, encouragement, fellowship and compassion.
- Christ can help us be intent on one purpose. He simplifies our focus. He shows us what is important and where to put our effort. But He doesn't force us. We have to choose His provision to be of the same mind, to maintain the same love, to be united in spirit, to be intent on one purpose.
- God rewards those who honor Him and don't selfishly step on others trying to find security. Christ is our example. He did not grasp at greatness and the security of being equal with God, but obeyed God the Father by becoming obedient to death. God rewards those who humbly trust and obey Him no matter how bleak things look.
- If you want to be great become a bond-servant to God. Greatness starts with a humble heart willing to do whatever God asks, even if it is embarrassing or doesn't seem in your best interest.

Challenges

- Am I of the same mind, spirit, love and purpose with other brothers and sisters in Christ?
- Am I taking advantage of the encouragement, love, affection, fellowship and compassion found in Christ?
- Am I intent on one purpose or do I have selfish ambition?
- Am I grasping at security with selfish ambition?
- Am I studying Christ as my example to find greatness?
- Am I willing to humbly trust and obey God even when things look bleak?
- Do I realize the path to greatness is through servanthood so all can achieve it?

Responses

- Father, help me focus on Your purpose for my current situation.
- Help me see that you are advancing your will when I am in a good situation and when I am in a bad situation.
- Help me learn the secret of being a servant.

Passage 5—Philippians 3:3-9

Facts

- We are the true circumcision.
- We worship in the Spirit of God.
- We glory in Christ Jesus.
- We put no confidence in our flesh.
- If anyone could be confident in his flesh, I (Paul) could more because...
- ...I was circumcised the 8th day,
- ...I am from the tribe of Benjamin,
- ...I am a Hebrew of Hebrews,
- ...A Pharisee of the Law,
- ...I am a zealous persecutor of the church,
- ...I am righteous and blameless according to the Law.
- But now, all that is worthless for the sake of Christ.
- Everything is worthless in comparison to knowing Christ Jesus as my Lord.
- I count everything as worthless in order to gain Christ.
- I want to be found in Him.
- Not having my own righteousness that comes from keeping the Law.
- I want a righteousness that comes through faith in Christ.
- I want a righteousness that comes from God because of my faith in Christ.

Lessons

- You don't need to have your own righteousness to gain Christ as your Lord. God does not want us to be confident in our ability to keep the rules in order to know Him as Lord. We can be a righteous rule keeper according to the Law, but that does not make us gain Christ. We have to get to the place where we realize all our abilities are worthless when it comes to gaining Christ.
- The goal is to be found in Christ with a righteousness that comes through faith in Christ.
- Paul says all of his best assets are worthless when compared to knowing Christ.

Challenges

- Is my confidence in my ability to be a righteous rule keeper, or in Christ's work?
- Do I really believe my salvation is about my faith in Christ's work, or do I still think I need to earn it?
- Do I realize my abilities are worthless apart from Christ?
- Am I seeking a righteousness that comes through faith in Christ, or through my own works?
- Do I think my strengths are worthless when compared to knowing Christ?
- What is most important to me? My abilities or knowing Christ?

Responses

- Father, help me to focus on You and not myself.

- Thank you for making a relationship with You possible.
- May my good behavior be motivated by love for You.

Passage 6—Philippians 3:17-21

Facts

- He wants his brethren to...
- ...follow his example,
- ...Watch those who walk according to this example,
- There are many who walk (he is saying this weeping) like this:
- ...They walk as enemies of the cross of Christ.
- ...Their end is destruction.
- ...Their god is their appetite.
- ...They glory in their shame.
- ...They set their mind on earthly things.
- Our citizenship is in heaven.
- We eagerly wait for a Savior, the Lord Jesus Christ.
- He will transform our humble body into conformity with His glorious body.
- He does this by exerting His power to subject all things to Himself.

Lessons

- God has given us examples to follow in His Word. We need to be careful to follow these examples because there are many who walk as enemies of the cross of Christ. They may talk like they are Christians, but they don't follow Christ.

- We can distinguish those who walk as enemies of the cross of Christ by their mindset and behavior. They are concerned with earthly things like success, power, money, and beauty. They are not eagerly waiting for their Savior, Jesus Christ, but glory in their own thinking and power to choose instead of God's ways. They think their desires and power are more important than understanding how to obey and conform to God's values.

- God will transform our humble body into conformity with His glorious body because He fixes everything under and around Himself. We won't always be flawed. Our job is to follow God's example, know our citizenship is not really here, but heaven, and eagerly wait for Him.

Challenges

- Am I following the examples that God has provided for me?
- Can I distinguish those who may talk like Christians, but really walk like His enemy?
- Am I eagerly waiting for Christ's return?
- Do I realize my citizenship is in heaven?

Responses

- Father, thank You for Your guidance while we are on earth.
- Please give me wisdom to recognize Your enemies and to not be influenced by them.
- May I always be clear that my citizenship is with You in heaven.
- Thank You for giving us so much to look forward to.

Passage 7—Philippians 4:4-7

Facts

- We should always rejoice in the Lord.
- It is important enough to repeat: Rejoice.
- Let everyone see your moderation.
- The Lord is at hand.
- Do not be anxious for anything.
- Instead, pray and ask, with thanksgiving, in every situation.
- Let God know your requests.
- The peace of God which surpasses all understanding, will guard your hearts and minds in Christ Jesus.

Lessons

- There is never a time where rejoicing IN THE LORD is inappropriate. Rejoicing in Him includes looking to Him for guidance. He is in control even when things seem to be going wrong.
- If we rejoice in the Lord, instead of our circumstances, we will not have unstable bouts of euphoria and depression depending on our situation. Our focus is on the Lord, not our circumstances. Everyone will see our moderation because we really believe the Lord is present in our life. God is not asking us to rejoice in bad circumstances, He wants us to rejoice that He can see us through "even this".
- Rejoicing does not mean we don't take responsibility for what is going wrong in our life. We rejoice in God's sovereignty, but we pray for wisdom to discern our part in every situation. We are thankful that God will lead us as we consult Him in prayer. This brings us peace. We are not alone in our problems.
- God doesn't want us to be anxious. He says in Ephesians 4:26 that we can be angry as long as we aren't sinning, but there is no place for anxiety. He is in charge. He will work all things together for good to those who love Him (Romans 8:28). He wants us to trust Him to lead us, as we consult Him. Fretting stems from wanting our own way. Calmness comes when we trust God's way.

Challenges

- Am I willing to rejoice in the Lord, no matter how bad things are going, because I believe He is good and able?
- Do I have my focus on the Lord, or on my circumstances?
- Do people see my moderation because I am fixed on the Lord, or do they see my erratic shifts as I go up and down according to my circumstances?
- Am I taking responsibility for what is not working in my life?
- Am I praying for wisdom to discern my part in every situation?
- Do I have peace because I consult God and trust Him to lead me?
- When I get anxious, am I willing to refocus on God and His ability to do what concerns me today?
- When I get anxious, am I willing to ask God for wisdom and courage to change what I need to change?
- Am I willing to accept God's will so that I can give up fretting and feel calm?

Responses

- Father, thank you for being bigger than my problems.

- Help me walk with You through life.

Passage 8—Philippians 4:8

Facts

- Finally, brothers and sisters, think on these things:
- Whatever is...
- ...true,
- ...honorable
- ...right
- ...pure
- ...lovely
- ...of good reputation
- ...excellent
- ...worthy of praise

Lessons

- God cares about our thought life. He wants us to dwell on uplifting, yet true, things.

Challenges

- Am I working on what I think about?
- Do I realize God thinks it is important?
- Am I making an effort to think about uplifting, yet true, things?

Responses

- Father, help me think about life from Your perspective. There is hope and joy from Your perspective.

Passage 9—Philippians 4:10-13, 18-19

Facts

- God so loved the world, that,
- He gave,
- His only Son, that,
- Whoever believes in Him,
- Would not perish,
- But, would have eternal life.
- God did not send the Son into the world to condemn the world.
- But to save the world.
- Through Jesus, He who believes in Him is not condemned.
- He who does not believe is already condemned, because, He does not believe in God's only Son.
- This is the condemnation: The Light came into the world, but men loved darkness rather than Light because their deeds were evil.

Lessons

- God so loves the world.

- God's response to seeing our condemnation and loving us, was to give His only Son to save us.
- God's gift of salvation is for anyone who believes in Christ's payment for them and wants it.
- God did not send Christ to condemn us, we were already condemned. Christ came to save us.
- Christ is the Light that came into the world.
- Those who love darkness hate the Light because their deeds are evil and light exposes them.

Challenges

- Do I see the heart of God's love for the world?
- Do I realize I was condemned and in peril before I accepted Christ's payment for my sins?
- Do I see how God offers salvation to all who want forgiveness instead of their dark sin?
- Do I live like Christ came to save me, not condemn me?
- Do I share Christ as the world's Light and hope?
- Do I continually choose Christ over sin?

Responses

- Father, thank You for loving us enough to save us from condemnation when we didn't first acknowledge that we were in trouble.
- Thank You for loving the world enough to send Your only Son to pay the price of forgiveness and warn us of our need.
- It is a spectacular gift where You pay the price, and we admit our sin and accept Christ's payment for it.
- You are a positive, loving, generous God Who sent Christ to save us when we were condemned already.

"If we speak
the truth about
His Son, God
can use us,
warts and all."

the Authors

www.ingramcontent.com/pod-product-compliance
Lightning Source LLC
Chambersburg PA
CBHW020517030426
42337CB00011B/424